Back Off, Sneezy!

▪ A KIDS' GUIDE TO STAYING WELL ▪

by Rachelle Kreisman

with illustrations by Tim Haggerty

RED
CHAIR
▪PRESS▪

Please visit our website at www.redchairpress.com for more high-quality products for young readers.

 For a free activity page for this story, go to
www.redchairpress.com and look for Free Activities.

Back Off Sneezy

Publisher's Cataloging-In-Publication Data
(Prepared by The Donohue Group, Inc.)

Kreisman, Rachelle, author.
Back off sneezy! : a kids' guide to staying well / by Rachelle Kreisman ; with illustrations by Tim Haggerty.

pages : illustrations ; cm. -- (Start smart: health)

Includes bibliographical references and index.

Summary: On a basketball. On a door handle. Even in the air you breathe! Germs are everywhere. What can you do about it? Learn ways to avoid germs, to guard against getting sick, and to keep from passing germs along to others.
ISBN: 978-1-937529-69-7 (library hardcover)
ISBN: 978-1-937529-68-0 (paperback)
ISBN: 978-1-937529-89-5 (ebook)

1. Health--Juvenile literature. 2. Health behavior--Juvenile literature. 3. Children--Health and hygiene--Juvenile literature. 4. Self-care, Health--Juvenile literature. 5. Health. 6. Children--Health and hygiene. 7. Self-care, Health. I. Haggerty, Tim, illustrator. II. Title.

RA777 .K742 2014

613/.0432   2013956244

Illustration credits: p. 1, 3, 5, 6, 7, 8, 11, 12, 13, 14, 15, 16, 17, 21, 22, 24, 25, 27, 29, 30, 31, 32: Tim Haggerty; p. 13: Mapping Specialists

Photo credits: Cover: © Blend Images/Alamy; p. 4, 5, 6, 7, 9, 10, 11, 12, 13, 14, 15, 17, 18, 20, 21, 24, 25, 26: IStock; p. 23: Dreamstime; p. 4, 5, 8: Shutterstock; p. 19: © Kidstock/Getty Images; p.32: Courtesy of the author, Rachel Kreisman

This series first published by:
Red Chair Press LLC   PO Box 333   South Egremont, MA 01258-0333

Printed in the United States of America

1 2 3 4 5 18 17 16 15 14

Table of Contents

Words in **bold type** are defined in the glossary.

CHAPTER 1

Germs!

Germs are tiny. They are so small you can't see them without a microscope. And they are everywhere! Some may live on you, and others in you. In fact, your body is home to *billions* of germs. Don't worry. Most of these teeny creatures cause no harm. Many can even help you. But some germs can make you sick. When they attack, your body fights them so you can get back to good health.

♥ You can't see them, but germs are all around you!

Your skin covers your body and protects you from germs. If you touch germs, your skin usually blocks them from doing harm.

But sometimes, germs do get into your body. They can creep in through openings. A cut on your skin is an entrance. Your mouth, nose, and eyes are like open doors that let some germs inside.

♥ Germs can get into your body. Cover a cleaned cut with an adhesive bandage to keep germs out and prevent infection.

Germs live in many places. Some germs may float in the air after someone sneezes. Others may live on things such as books, toys, computers, just about everywhere. So when you touch something with germs on it, they can stay on your hands.

If that happens, those yucky germs on your hands may make you sick. All you need to do is touch your mouth, nose, or eyes. The germs may enter your body.

Your hands may carry germs from one place to another.

What happens next? Your body gets busy trying to get rid of the germs. First, they have to get past some obstacles set up by your body to fight them. Did germs just crawl inside your nose? Then they have to get past nose hairs and **mucus**. The slimy liquid traps germs. When you blow your nose or sneeze, the germs come out.

♥ Using a tissue traps the mucus and germs when you blow your nose.

You also have mucus in your mouth and lungs. A cough can send the germs flying out. Saliva and tears can break down germs and wash them away. Blood from a cut can wash germs out too. Acid in your stomach can also kill germs.

Your body has a good first line of defense. But some germs can still sneak in. If that happens, you may get sick. But have no fear—your **immune system** is here!

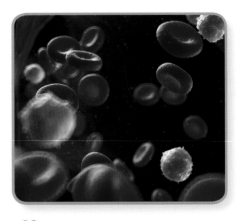

Your immune system fights against germ invaders. Special cells work for your immune

♥ White blood cells are the body's defenders. They fight germs.

system. They are white blood cells. They find and destroy germs. You may feel sick during this time. After the germs are gone, you start to feel better.

Your body also makes **antibodies** to remember the germs. If the same kinds of germs come back, watch out! Your body can quickly destroy them before you feel sick.

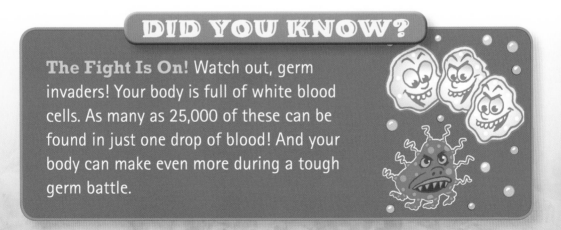

DID YOU KNOW?

The Fight Is On! Watch out, germ invaders! Your body is full of white blood cells. As many as 25,000 of these can be found in just one drop of blood! And your body can make even more during a tough germ battle.

Not all germs are the same. Some germs are called **bacteria**. Most bacteria are good. A few kinds of bacteria are nasty, though. They can cause illnesses such as **strep throat** and ear infections.

Viruses are another kind of germ. There are more than 100 different viruses that cause colds and the **flu**. Those two illnesses pass easily from person to person. When a sick person sneezes or coughs, germs fly out. They spread through the air. You can get sick if you breathe the germ-filled air. That's why people cover their mouths when they sneeze or cough. It helps keep virus germs from spreading.

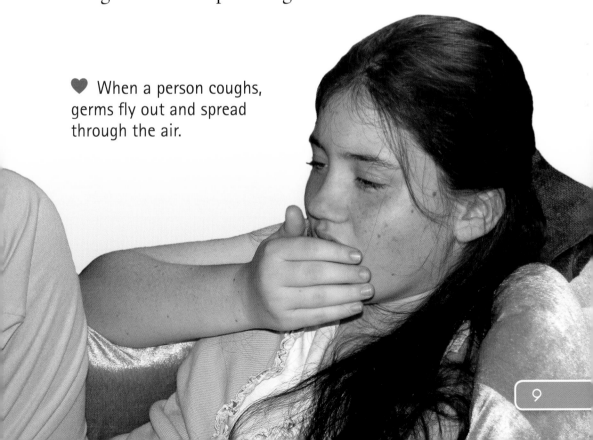

♥ When a person coughs, germs fly out and spread through the air.

CHAPTER 2

You Can Help

Your body works hard to keep you healthy. Don't let your body do all the work. You can help too. What is the best way to keep from getting sick? Wash your hands often with soap and water. That will send germs down the drain. Always wash after you use the bathroom. Wash before you prepare or eat food, too.

Wash well! Rub your soapy hands together for 15 to 20 seconds. Be sure to wash between fingers and under your nails. (Germs can hide there.) Also suds up your wrists and the backs of your hands. Hello, clean hands! Goodbye, germs.

♥ Be sure to use soap when washing your hands. Soap can help get rid of germs.

Remember, germs can creep in through openings. Don't let those germs in! Avoid touching your nose, mouth, and eyes if your hands aren't clean. Think twice before you put your finger in your mouth. Wash your hands first! And always use a tissue to clean your dry or runny nose.

♥ Think twice before putting your hands in your mouth.

TRY THIS!

How will you know if you did a good job washing? Sing the "Happy Birthday" song twice or the "Alphabet Song" once as you wash. That is just the right amount of time to get hands clean and germ-free. Then be sure to dry them completely.

♥ Getting a flu vaccine once a year can protect you all year.

Colds and flu are easy to catch. But the flu is much more serious. It can make you feel awful. What can you do to prevent it? Experts say to get the flu **vaccine** (vak-SEEN) each fall. It is often given as a shot. The vaccine protects your body from the flu.

How do vaccines work? Most contain germs that are weak or dead. They do not give you a disease. They help your body to prepare for one.

DID YOU KNOW?

Vaccines are germ fighters that prevent many serious diseases— the measles, chicken pox, and mumps, to name a few.

Let's say your doctor gives you a vaccine as a shot or by mouth. You know about it, but your immune system has no clue. In fact, your body thinks it is under attack. It makes antibodies for that kind of germ. If the actual germ ever invades, your body is ready. Antibodies remember the germ and can quickly destroy it.

♥ Regular check-ups with your doctor should be part of your wellness plan.

What else can you do to avoid germs? Try to stay away from people who are sick. This can be tricky if someone you live with has a cold or other virus. So wash your hands more often during this time. Be sure to wash them after you touch items that sick family members touch. For example, if you share a TV remote control, wash your hands after using it. If a friend is sick, try not to get too close either.

♥ Germs can be easily spread by sharing household items.

♥ Sharing is a great idea but sharing your germs is never good.

Sharing with others is wonderful. Sharing germs is not. Don't share plates, drinking glasses, spoons, or forks. If you do, you could also be sharing germs!

Practice This:

1. A friend is drinking a glass of orange juice. It sure looks yummy. And you are very thirsty. She asks, "Would you like a sip?" What do you say?

2. Your cousin is eating a bowl of your favorite cereal. It looks so good. He holds out his spoon with some cereal on it. "Have some," he says. What do you say?

In both cases say, "No, thanks!" Instead, get your own bowl of cereal or glass of juice and enjoy!

CHAPTER 3

Sick Days

Here's the good news—you tried your best to avoid harmful germs. The bad news is that you got sick anyway. It can happen. Now you can focus on getting well again. Here are some things that can help you get better:

* Stay home and get lots of rest.

* Gargle with salt water if you have a sore throat.

* Ask a grown up if you should use a saline spray to clear a stuffy nose.

* Drink plenty of water. Tea, soup, and other warm drinks are good too. Liquids help loosen thick mucus.

* Eat small meals even if you are not hungry.

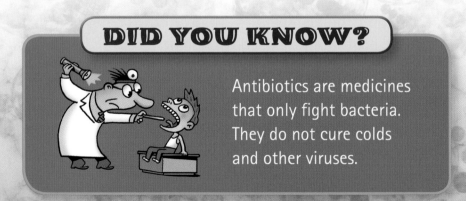

DID YOU KNOW?

Antibiotics are medicines that only fight bacteria. They do not cure colds and other viruses.

Sometimes, you may need to go to a doctor. He or she will examine you and decide if you need medicine. You may need to take an **antibiotic**. That medicine helps your body destroy bad bacteria. Two infections caused by bacteria are strep throat and ear infections.

Always finish all of the antibiotics the doctor tells you to take. If not, your body may not get rid of all of the bad bacteria.

♥ If you don't feel well, a doctor may examine you to determine how best to help you feel better.

Being sick may make your body temperature rise. That is called fever. Normal body temperature is around 98.6 degrees F.

Fever helps your body fight infections. You may feel hot and sweaty. You may also shiver and feel cold. If your fever is too high, your doctor may want you to take medicine to lower it.

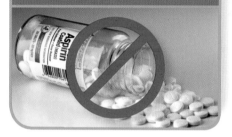
TRY THIS!

Ask a grown-up to help take your temperature at different times during the day. Record your results. Your temperature can change throughout the day. A normal range may be from 97 to 99 degrees F. Does it go up, down, or stay the same during the day?

Do you feel a sneeze coming on? Try to cover your mouth with a tissue. If you can't get a tissue in time, bend your arm and bring it to your mouth. Then sneeze into the place where it bends. *Achoo!* Send coughs into the bend of your arm too. If you cough or sneeze into your hands, you may spread germs to others.

Catch that runny nose! Blow your nose into a tissue to clear the mucus. Germs exit your body that way. After you blow your nose, throw the tissue away. Then wash your hands to send those germs down the drain.

Cover your nose and mouth when you sneeze, please!

CHAPTER 4 Stay Healthy

Being sick is no fun. Your body is working hard to fight off enemy germs. The battle will not last for too long. You may feel better in a day or two. Sometimes it can take longer to get well. If it does, hang in there!

Your body needs rest when you are sick.

Once you are feeling better, smile! The hard part is over. Now you can focus on staying healthy. Practice healthy habits every day. That will help keep your body in tip-top shape for fighting germs.

What are healthy habits? They include staying clean, eating well, and drinking water. Getting enough exercise and sleep are also important. *Haha!* Laughing is great too. Keep reading to find out why.

♥ Being active can help your body fight germs.

Good **hygiene** (HI-gene) means keeping your body clean to stay healthy. You already know how important it is to wash your hands. The rest of your body needs to be cleaned too. Take baths or showers to wash off dirt, sweat and bacteria. If you don't bathe often, your skin can get infected.

Bacteria live inside your mouth too. Some bacteria can damage teeth and gums. Get rid of the bad bacteria. How? Brush your teeth at least twice a day—in the morning and before bedtime. Gently brush your tongue. Use **floss** once a day to clean between teeth. Have an adult make sure you are flossing and brushing correctly.

How else can you stay healthy? Kids need to be active for at least one hour each day. Being active helps to keep your body strong and healthy. Exercise also helps burn fat. That keeps your body at a good weight. Having a healthy weight helps prevent illness. So get moving!

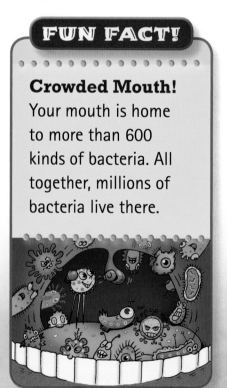

FUN FACT!

Crowded Mouth!
Your mouth is home to more than 600 kinds of bacteria. All together, millions of bacteria live there.

Play tag or soccer, ride a bike, jump rope, run, or dance. Choose activities you like and have fun.

Laughter is also good for you. It reduces **stress**. Stress is the body's way of reacting when you are worried. Too much stress is bad for your immune system. Laughing can make you feel happy. If you are having a bad day, try to laugh.

♥ Exercise can be more fun with a friend.

Eat a variety of healthful foods. Each food has different **nutrients**. Nutrients help your body grow and heal. They also give you energy. Munch on lots of vegetables and fruits. Say "yes" to whole grains, such as oatmeal and plain popcorn. Eat meat, fish, and beans. Snack on low-fat milk, yogurt, and cheese.

Drink lots of water too. Sip water regularly through-out the day. Take extra water breaks when you exercise and on hot days.

♥ Choose food wisely to build a strong body.

FUN FACT!

People can live up to eight weeks without food. They can only live from three to five days without water.

It has been a long day. Are you feeling sleepy? You may need to get to bed earlier. Most school-age kids need 10 to 11 hours of sleep each night. Getting enough shut-eye helps keep you healthy and do better at school. Sleep lets your body and brain rest. Your immune system works best after a good night's sleep. If you don't get enough sleep, your body has a harder time fighting germs.

♥ As you grow into your teenage years, your changing body may need more sleep.

Now you know lots of ways to take good care of yourself to stay healthy. Of course, you don't need to practice every healthy habit at the same time. You can't eat your veggies while you brush your teeth. And you can't sneeze into your arm while you are jumping rope.

But knowing where germs come from and how to stay away from them will keep you healthy and happy.

What You Can Do!

How many of these rules do you follow?
Count the number of things you do.
How did you do? See how you score below.

You...

1 wash your hands before you eat.

2 sneeze into a tissue or the bend of your arm.

3 stay home and rest if you are sick.

4 exercise for an hour each day.

5 brush your teeth twice a day.

6 eat a variety of healthy foods.

7 drink water throughout the day.

8 get plenty of sleep each night.

9 take baths or showers regularly.

10 make laughter a part of your life.

If you answered "yes" to...

* **eight or more**—Great job staying healthy!

* **five to seven**—You are almost there.

* **one to four**—Keep trying. You can do it!

Glossary

antibiotic: medicine that destroys bacteria

antibodies: something the body makes to attack harmful germs

bacteria: a kind of germ

floss: thread that cleans between teeth and along the gums

flu: an illness caused by a virus

hygiene: keeping clean to stay healthy

immune system: the body system that protects against harmful germs

mucus: a slimy liquid produced by parts of the body

nutrients: the good things found in food that people need to grow and live

organ: a part of the body that helps the body function

strep throat: a throat infection caused by bacteria

stress: the body's way of reacting when a person is worried

vaccine: something put into the body to prevent disease

virus: a kind of germ that causes disease

What Did You Learn?

See how much you learned about staying healthy.
Answer *true* or *false* for each statement below.
Write your answers on a separate piece of paper.

1 Germs can enter your body through your nose.
True or false?

2 Some fevers make your body temperature drop.
True or false?

3 White blood cells are part of your immune system.
True or false?

4 Many kinds of bacteria live inside your mouth.
True or false?

5 Washing your hands may often spread germs.
True or false?

Answers: 1. True, 2. False (Fevers make your body temperature rise.), 3. True, 4. True, 5. False (Washing your hands prevents the spread of germs.)

For More Information

Books

Here are some books you might like to read. Check your school's media center for these and other books about staying healthy.

Burstein, John. *Staying Well* (Slim Goodbody's Good Health Guides). Gareth Stevens Publishing, 2007.

Fromer, Liza. *My Healthy Body.* Tundra Books, 2012.

Gray, Shirley Wimbish. *Exercising for Good Health* (Living Well). The Child's World, 2004.

Green, Jen. *Skin, Hair, and Hygiene* (Your Body and Health). Aladdin Books Ltd, 2006.

Parker, Steve. *Microlife That Helps Us* (Amazing World of Microlife). Raintree, 2006.

Senker, Cath. *Keeping Clean* (Healthy Choices). Powerkids Press, 2008.

Web Sites

BAM! Body and Mind: Hand Washing:
http://www.cdc.gov/bam/body/buzz-scuzz.html

BAM! Body and Mind: Immune System:
http://www.cdc.gov/bam/diseases/immune

KidsHealth: Immune Cells (movie):
http://kidshealth.org/kid/htbw/ISmovie.html

Microbe Magic: http://microbemagic.ucc.ie

Scrub Club: http://www.scrubclub.org

Note to educators and parents: Our editors have carefully reviewed these web sites to ensure they are suitable for children. Web sites change frequently, however, and we cannot guarantee that a site's future contents will continue to meet our high standards of quality and educational value. You may wish to preview these sites and closely supervise children whenever they access the Internet.

Index

About the Author

Rachelle Kreisman has been a children's writer and editor for many years. She wrote hundreds of classroom magazines for *Weekly Reader*. Those issues included health topics about nutrition, illness prevention, sports safety, and fitness. When Rachelle is not writing, she enjoys being active. She likes taking walks, hiking, biking, kayaking, and doing yoga.